START-UP
RELIGION
BELONGING

Ruth Nason

Evans

Published by Evans Brothers Limited
2A Portman Mansions
Chiltern Street
London W1U 6NR

© Evans Brothers Limited 2005

Produced for Evans Brothers Limited by
White-Thomson Publishing Ltd,
Bridgewater Business Centre,
210 High Street,
Lewes, East Sussex BN7 2NH

Printed in China by WKT Co. Ltd.

Consultants: Jean Mead, Senior Lecturer in Religious
Education, School of Education, University of
Hertfordshire; Dr Anne Punter, Partnership Tutor,
School of Education, University of Hertfordshire.
Designer: Carole Binding

Cover: All photographs by Chris Fairclough

The right of Ruth Nason to be identified as the author of
this work has been asserted by her in accordance with the
Copyright, Designs and Patents Act 1988.

British Library Cataloguing in Publication Data
Nason, Ruth
    Belonging - (Start-up religion)
    1. Religions - Juvenile literature
    I. Title
    200

ISBN: 0 237 527642

Acknowledgements:
Special thanks to the following for their help and
involvement in the preparation of this book: Angie and
Duncan and the girls, the Buckler family, the Harden
family, Heather Lees, the Petevinos family, the Rajan
family, Sharon Smith, the Skillman family, the Wise
family, Rev. Graham Clarke, Rev. Christopher Futcher,
the Imam and congregation of the Jamia Mosque,
Watford, the congregation of High Street Methodist
Church, Harpenden, the congregation of Upper Tooting
Methodist Church.

Picture Acknowledgements:
Art Directors/TRIP: pages 13 (H. Rogers), 17 (K.
Cardwell); Circa Photo Library (B. J. Mistry): page 6
(bottom); Chris Fairclough Colour Library: page 9;
Michael Nason: pages 12 (bottom), 16; World Religions
Photo Library: page 11.
All other photographs by Chris Fairclough.

Contents

Think about belonging

▼ **Stephen and his brothers belong to a club.
How can you tell what kind of club it is?**

Which club do you belong to?

belong   club

► **Gemma's uniform shows that she belongs to Beavers. She has made the Beaver promise.**

I promise to do my best, to be kind and helpful and to love God.

◄ **Taribo is wearing his school uniform. How do your teachers like you to behave when you are in your uniform?**

uniform   promise   God   behave   **5**

Belonging to a family

What does it feel like to belong to a family? Here are some ideas.

We care about each other.

We know each other very well.

family   care

Mum loves us, even when we get home muddy.

There are things that we all remember.

We celebrate special times together.

I'm learning to play like my dad.

loves   remember   celebrate 7

Belonging to a religion

▶ Jenny, Emma and their mum belong to the Christian religion. Jenny is learning to pray to God.

◀ Samuel is Jewish. He wears a special hat when he prays. This shows respect for God.

Christian   religion   pray   Jewish

In many religions people believe in a God, who knows everything. Religions also have rules, to help the people know the right things to do.

People in the Sikh religion have a rule never to cut their hair. It is like wearing a uniform.

Special times

In some religions, one day of the week is a special day. People meet on that day to worship and think about God.

▶ On Sundays, many Christians go to church. Singing is often a part of the worship.

◀ Friday is a special day for Muslims to pray at the mosque.

worship   church   Muslims

Like families, religions have times each year when everyone celebrates an important event.

▲ In the Hindu religion there is a festival for the birthday of a god called Krishna. What days do you celebrate?

mosque   Hindu   festival   god 11

Welcoming someone new

▶ It was a special day when Gemma joined Beavers. Do you remember the promise she made? (See page 5.)

◀ It is also a special time when someone new comes into a family.

What can people in a family do to welcome a new baby?

joined   welcome   ceremony

Some religions have a ceremony to welcome a baby.

▶ In the Buddhist religion, many families take their babies to be blessed by a monk. The monk flicks water over the baby and prays that the baby's life will be safe and good.

What wishes would you make for a new baby?

Buddhist   blessed   monk   13

Baptising a baby

This is Benjamin. His parents wanted him to be welcomed into the Christian religion. They took him to their church for a ceremony called a baptism.

They had chosen two people to be godparents for Benjamin.

► They all made promises to help him learn about being Christian.

baptism   godparents

► The **minister** used some olive oil to draw a **cross** on Benjamin's head. A cross is a **sign** of the Christian religion.

◄ At the **font**, the minister splashed water on Benjamin's head.

He said that God had now welcomed Benjamin as part of the Christian religion.

minister   cross   sign   font   **15**

A different ceremony

There are many different Christian churches. They do not all have baptisms like the one on pages 14-15.

◀ This is another little boy called Ben, with his family. Their church had a dedication ceremony to welcome Ben.

▶ The minister held Ben and everyone promised to help bring him up as a Christian.

dedication

Ben's parents hope that, when he grows up, he will decide to have a believer's baptism.

Believer's baptism is for grown-ups. They promise to be Christians for all their life.

► The minister dips the person under the water and helps them come up again. This is to show that the person is starting a new life as a Christian.

decide   believer's baptism   17

Growing up

Children learn to be part of their religion in many ways. They take part in worship and festivals (pages 10-11).

◀ They join in customs at home, like singing a Jewish thankyou prayer for food.

▶ They help to care for people in need. Sometimes they give money to help them.

customs   prayer   in need

► They go to classes. For example, Muslim children go to classes at the mosque, to learn to read their holy book.

◄ These children belong to a Junior Church. They are learning about a special meal of bread and wine that many Christians share.

How are you learning to belong to your school or family?

holy book   Junior Church   share   19

What's special about belonging?

Belonging makes a **difference** to people's lives.

I play football with my team.

I work together with friends in my class.

difference   team

What do you belong to? How does belonging help to make you feel special?

Hebrew

Further information for

New words introduced in the text:

baptism	care	decide	godparents	minister	respect
behave	celebrate	dedication	Hebrew	monk	rules
believe	ceremony	difference	Hindu	mosque	share
believer's	Christian	family	holy book	Muslims	sign
baptism	church	festival	in need	pray	Sikh
belong	club	font	Jewish	prayer	team
blessed	cross	God	joined	promise	uniform
Buddhist	customs	god	Junior Church	religion	welcome
			loves	remember	worship

Background Information

This book shows examples from a range of religions. Teachers are likely to base activities on examples from the religions represented in their class or school (e.g. if there are Greek Orthodox children, include their baptism ceremonies).
Be aware of children who might feel left out if they do not belong to a religion, and select activities that they can relate to. Also be aware of the danger of stereotypes and generalisations. Preface statements with words like 'some/many Christians' etc.

Belonging is an excellent topic through which to build relationships with families and local faith communities. A letter home explaining the topic, with a non-intrusive approach, may produce offers of home videos, cards, artefacts, parents willing to talk or be questioned, or even an invitation for small, supervised groups of children to visit a home and find clues about the religion the family belongs to. Ensure that people who talk about their religion are clear about the focus, and the protocols of talking to a non-religious audience.
Page 8: You may want to talk about what Christians wear. The cross is a Christian symbol, but it is often used in jewellery without implying Christian commitment. Lapel badges of a cross, or a fish symbol, are more significant.

Page 10: Hindus and Sikhs do not have a weekly holy day but usually meet at weekends for convenience.
Page 12: Circumcision is one of the ceremonies for Jewish and Muslim boy babies, so think how (or whether) to deal with this.
Page 14: Baptism is the religious ceremony, also known as christening. The baptism of Jesus is in Luke 3. 21-22. The symbolism of baptism is explained in Romans 6. 3-5.
Page 19: Weekend classes often take place in churches, Hindu temples, synagogues and gurdwaras. In mosques, daily after-school classes are called madrasahs. Children learn about holy books and religious practice and there is often language and cultural support for children of ethnic-minority communities.

Suggested Activities

PAGES 4-5

Ask children about groups they belong to. Have a 'uniform day': children come in uniform and tell about their group/club.
Display a class photo headed 'WE ALL BELONG TO …'.
Examine the school badge/motto.
Discuss feelings about and implications of belonging. Do you belong even when not wearing the uniform?

Parents and Teachers

PAGES 6-7

Make a display of children's paintings of their families.
Let the children complete a family tree or 'important people in my life' diagram.
Let small groups of children dress up and role-play families, showing activities they enjoy together or caring for each other.

PAGES 8-9

Talk about religions that children and teachers belong to. Begin a religions display, with name/symbols/pictures. Discuss that some children belong to a religion, and let them tell how they show this (symbols/behaviour). Show artefacts or pictures of items that show belonging to a religion. Add them to the display.

PAGES 10-11

Let children tell about their experiences of going to places of worship. Add names and pictures of buildings, and names of days of worship, to the religions display.
Discuss in what ways school assemblies are similar to this.

PAGES 12-13

Ask children to demonstrate their clubs' joining ceremonies. Jointly devise a ceremony to welcome a new child to the class. Ask a family how they prepared for and welcomed a new baby. By means of a visitor/video/pictures, tell about initiation ceremonies of the religions of the children in the class. Let the children re-enact an initiation, using a baby doll.

PAGES 14-15

Show a video of a baptism. Let children tell of any baptisms they have been to. Display christening cards, presents, gowns, candles, certificates. Role-play a baptism ceremony, with a clergyman and in a church if possible. Discuss the promises made by the family, godparents and church. How will people keep the promises as the baby grows up? Discuss the promises parents and school make when a child joins the school.

PAGES 16-17

Arrange a visit from or to a church that practises believer's baptism, or show a video of a dedication and adult baptism. Discuss promises made on joining a club. Make a list of good promises to make when joining a class, and all sign it in a little ceremony. What promises would an adult make when joining a religion? Why is it good to have a ceremony to show this?

PAGES 18-19

Let children tell what they do in classes at places of worship. Make a list of ways religious families remind themselves about God (e.g. mezuzahs, pictures, shrines, texts, prayers, books, food rules). Add pictures of these to the religions display.

PAGES 20-21

Let children find the earlier pictures in the book about the children on this spread and say what they learned about them. Let children draw pictures of themselves in the middle of concentric circles, showing all the groups they belong to. Use ICT graphics to make 'I am special' shields or children's initials filled with pictures of what is special in their life.

23

Index